GOALS DONE

#	GOAL	DATE
4	WIN A SAILING RACE	1969
15	DO A PARACHUTE JUMP	1985
22*	FLY A GLIDER 200KM	1993
25	SKI A BLACK RUN	1998
32	RIDE A MOTORBIKE AT 125MPH	2003
44	RUN COMRADES 90 KM	2007/8
67	AMAZON BESTSELLER	2016
80	RACE IRONMAN	2013
85	GET A TATTOO	2013
89	SAIL ACROSS ATLANTIC	2019
90	RUN 100 MILES	2016
96	DIVE WITH SHARKS	2012
98	PARAGLIDE AT 10.000 FT	2015
106	VISIT 50 COUNTRIES	2019

Those Were FUN !

JUNE 2020

Published by
Nigel J Wall Publishing
Warwick, CV34 6AR, UK
www.live-life-now.com

ISBN: 978-1-5272-6572-1

Contact details

Email the author at nigel@live-life-now.com

Read more about Live Life Now and the author at

www.live-life-now.com

Dedication

To my Daughters Kath, Anna and Vivian and my forever best friend, coach, editor, critic and hero, Giselle Hudson.

Thanks for the inspiration!

"After reading Nigel's book, I was inspired to get up off the sofa & finish those tricky two chapters of my book that have been waiting to be completed for quite a while!"
Pamela, Managing Director, London, England

"I went from a backwater sales rep to CEO of an international technology company in less than 10 years following Nigel's coaching and philosophies!"
Matt, Chief Executive Officer, Houston, USA

"It's the kind of book that can change your life if you'll let it, all in a fun and easy to read format that will make you want to!"
Racquel, CEO, Port of Spain, Trinidad

Foreword

I have occasionally wondered to myself how Nigel Wall finds time to work and what he does to earn the amazing lifestyle he lives. I cannot recall ever seeing him promote his services on social media. Mostly I see pictures of him participating in cool adventures, fun events, and ultra-challenging athletic competitions.

Nigel starts "Live Life Now" with a fascinating and impressive list of goals that he has already accomplished, and I know he will continue to reach whatever goals he sets out to achieve in the future.

He turned his physical, mental, career, and financial life totally around by making important decisions about his purpose and goals, and taking consistent, daily, actions. It is just that simple but not that simple.

"Live Life Now" provides you with a detailed, action oriented, process, system, and action plans to help you pursue your purpose and achieve your goals in every area of your life, whatever they may be. That is a very bold statement, but it is 100% true.

Being the world's most well-known Napoleon Hill Foundation's Certified Instructor, I know a lot about the 17 universal success principles that Hill identified during his 25 years of research. Napoleon Hill, at the request of Andrew Carnegie, one of the wealthiest men who ever lived, studied the most successful people of his day including Thomas Edison, Henry Ford, William Wrigley Jr., King Gillette, F.W. Woolworth, Theodore Roosevelt, and Wilbur Wright. This book covers many of the results that Hill found in successful people.

"Live Life Now" provides you with everything you need to decide what you want to accomplish with your life and what actions are required to tick those goals off your list. Will it be easy? Definitely not. Is it worth it? I guarantee you that it is. Will following the ideas in this book get you there? I know for sure that they will because I have used them as well.

Life may even get more challenging than it is now. If you truly want to change and have a burning desire to get the most out of your life, you will encounter adversities and challenges along the way.

To pursue your purpose and goals, you will have to do a lot of things you don't feel like doing, when you don't feel like doing them. That is most of the key to success right there.

Life is going to be challenging no matter what happens, and you will have to do things you don't feel like doing, whether you strive for success, or accept mediocrity. If you're going to have to do things you don't feel like doing, at least choose to do things that will make you a better person.

By deciding upon a purpose and goals for your life, your challenges will mostly be of your own choosing, and will make you a better person in everything you do. Being hard on yourself makes life easier for you in the long run. "Live Life Now" is an easy to follow guide that will challenge you to be your best self and bring joy and happiness to you and your loved ones. It is simple to follow but can be challenging to execute.

The other key to success is best summarized by Napoleon Hill, "Whatever your mind can conceive and believe, your mind can achieve". Purposefully choosing and managing your 60,000 daily thoughts, and taking action on a daily basis, will ensure that you achieve any goal you set, provided you NEVER EVER give up.

Make the decision to Live Life Now and I know that I will see you at the top!

Tom 'too tall' Cunningham
Napoleon Hill Foundation Certified Instructor
International Motivational Speaker
Creator of the International Bestselling Journeys to Success book series

Note from author Nigel J Wall

Sadly, my friend Tom passed away before this book was published. His widow, Kim Cunningham, gave us permission to use his wise words as part of his legacy of leadership in personal and professional achievement.

Contents

Introduction

There seems to be a whole world of living out there that few of us take full advantage of. If we do realise it, often we are already on a path that makes it seem too hard to change and so we do the easy thing, which is nothing. Shame isn't it? With all of that incredible potential, we settle for second best and go through life failing to live up to our greatest potential.

The barriers that hold us back are almost all internal: our conditioning, our environment and current circumstances often prevent us from thinking about changing, let alone taking action.

Each chapter in this guide takes one of those 'holdbacks', from 'not enough time' to 'not able to' and everything in-between and provides ideas and action steps to break it down and remove these obstacles, once and for all!

One of the most fundamental changes that we can make lies in the awareness of 1440 and how we spend it.

You do understand the 1440, don't you? The number of minutes in the day! We all get 1440. If you are rich, you get 1440, and if you are poor you get 1440. You can't buy, sell, save until later, or get back minutes if you are wasteful so you had better be ultra-careful about how you use your daily allotted 1440!

There is no magic in getting the best out of 1440, but there are steps that will guide you towards achieving the things you want and making the most out of them!

After each chapter you will find an Action Plan with exercises to help you create your own success blueprint and reinforce the ideas learned. There are also notes pages at the back of the book to write random thoughts and ideas so this book becomes your 'go to' place for your life plans.

Einstein once defined insanity as "doing the same thing over and over again and expecting a different result." Don't fall into the insanity trap – reading to get wiser. Learn, apply, do different things or do things differently and I guarantee you will get much better results and learn how to Live Life Now!

Nigel J Wall
June 2020

1. Dream Large

"If you don't have a dream, then how are you going to make a dream come true?"
Oscar Hammerstein

Remember when you were a child and people asked you what you wanted to be when you grew up? Think of all those great things that went through your mind:

- an Olympic champion
- an airline pilot
- an actor
- a fireman
- a singer
- a pro footballer
- a model
- a famous writer
- a comedian
- a millionaire
- and maybe even an astronaut!

Then maybe your parents, relatives or friends brought you back down from the height of your dream with a thud, reminding you that your dreams were unrealistic or even stupid fantasies and that accountancy, engineering, law, nursing or virtually anything else would be the right thing for you to do. Much more sensible than wanting to be an astronaut, eh?

Did you know that the USA alone has produced some 340 astronauts since NASA started operating? Did you also know that you can apply on the NASA website to join that elite core? Additionally there are international and Russian astronauts which push that number to over 800.

Ask Lt. Col. (ret) Catherine (Cady) Coleman about what it's like to be an astronaut. She doesn't say it's easy. In fact, she says: "The biggest challenge about being involved in the space program is the need to be able to be good at, and know, a lot about a lot of things". That doesn't mean that you can't do it or that it's a stupid dream. It just takes dedication and commitment! Cady has spent many months in space on a number of different shuttle missions and has had many 'firsts' as an astronaut, mostly science-related but there is one first that was both unique and unusual: she played a flute duet with rock musician Ian Anderson where she was on the space station and he was in a concert hall in Russia! What a phenomenal first!

It's always a good idea to dream but an even better idea when dreaming is to dream large!

Dreaming large requires you to shift from your current position, shake off your conditioning and imagine that you can really achieve anything that you want to, when you truly reach out and use more of your potential which comprises of the following:

- Mental/intellectual – How much of your mental capacity do you think you use on a daily basis? Maybe you're guessing 10% to 15% right? Well that is somewhat of a myth. Our brains are very busy almost all of the time so the real answer is close to 100%. However how we use that resource and what we can do to develop It further is a fact. The good news is that you can train your brain to increase your mental and intellectual potential. Take for example Joshua Foer: from a basic start of not remembering where his car keys were or any of his friend's phone numbers, he trained to improve his memory and in one year he became the American memory champion! And then there is Preston Ely who decided he wanted to join the elite Mensa group, (the largest and oldest high IQ society in the world), making up the top 2% of the general population on an approved intelligence test that has been properly administered and supervised. He benchmarked at 'you're average' on an online test and then went to the brain gym where after 3 months, was rated at 'genius' level. More on 'how to do that' later but in the meantime - go workout your brain!

- Physical – How fit are you? How energised, are you and how well do you look after yourself? We have an incredible physical potential that can enable us to achieve amazing feats. These achievements can help us and positively influence all areas of our lives including our happiness, attitude, energy, mental activity and, of course our health. Even if you regularly workout you may only be using a small percentage of your full potential. One of Preston Ely's core 'secrets' to getting smart was a rigorous cardiovascular exercise regime. I like to test things and not simply rely on stories told by others, so I decided to see how far I could run and ride a bike. In 2013 I rode a bicycle 300 miles in 23 hours and in 2014 I ran 101 miles in 29 hours. You don't have to do what I do, but you could if you decided to!

- Emotional – Our emotional potential is all about our feelings. That fluffy stuff that can't really be measured, but we can certainly tell when we are happy and when we are not! How we use and develop it is actually something that we can control. Like changing your job from something you dislike to something you love can work wonders for your happiness. Start simply. Write down a list of all the things that you love to do and spend more of your time doing those things!

- Spiritual/ethical – whatever your belief system is, it is often how you live your life and that you do things that really matter, rather than purely taking random action. Your value system and beliefs can be a huge benefit to you as you guide yourself on your life's journey.

So given that we are now in a position to really unleash our potential it is time to dream and I mean, dream large!

Dream – regular	Dream – large
Learn to fly	Own my own plane
Get a beach house	..on an island in the Caribbean
Be self employed	Own my own business
Be fit	Win a marathon
Write a book	Be a bestselling author
Pass my exams	Get an MBA or Doctorate
Travel the world	Go to the moon!
Have a great job..	...that I love to do!
Help others	Change the world!

You may look at this list and think "these are some pretty wild dreams!" However that depends on your view and starting point. What you will find later on in this book, is the amazing things you can achieve when you follow some really simple steps.

To truly 'dream large' you don't have to worry about being five again; all you need is a pad of paper, a pen or pencil and a clear mind. Forget everything about 'now', close your eyes and dream of all of the things you really want to achieve in your life, then open your eyes and start writing and keep writing! If you run out of ideas then take a break and start again later. If you've filled a page then start a new one. If you've filled the pad then congratulate yourself! When you have written everything down, then sit back, relax and figure where you are going to start.

Sounds crazy? Consider this: in 1940 when 15 year old John Goddard couldn't decide what to do with his life he took a pad and pen and wrote down everything he wanted to achieve in his life. His list consisted of 127 goals from milking a rattlesnake, landing and taking off from an aircraft carrier, to visiting every country in the world. He managed to achieve 109 of them in his incredible, adventurous lifetime!

I'm not quite up to 127, but my personal life list comprises over 100 major goals and I've achieved well over 70 of those goals. You are actually reading goal #51 right now! One thing I can personally guarantee is if you follow the process, it really works!

When you've done your 'dream large' list on the next page and figured out where to start, then read on!

Plan 1 - Dreaming

My Personal 'Dream Large' List

Name: _________________________________Date: _______________

#	Dream	Priority

2. Have Goals

"Set your goals high, and don't stop 'til you get there!"
Bo Jackson, Athlete

This comes in high on the wisdom list because, as you may have already heard - if you don't know where you are going, any road will take you there! Many of us have dreams, wishes and desires, but how many have clear concise goals written down and goals that you're actually working on? You see, goals are dreams with a deadline and action plan, but an unwritten goal is just a 'wish'. The following are examples of dreams and wishes:

- To lose weight

- To improve qualifications

- To be wealthy

- To retire early

- To get fit

- To have a beach house

- To get an ideal job

- To help others

Why are these dreams and desires and not goals? Easy answer: they are not specific! There is no deadline and almost certainly no written action plan. Without these three components it is highly unlikely that you'll have the motivation to achieve anything on your goal list. Any achievement of yours will depend solely on luck. Without specific deadlines and a written action plan, how will you know when you've reached your goal?

- Is 'lose weight' 5lbs this year or 15lbs over the next 3 months?

- I can improve qualifications by getting a degree. Is that an MBA or a PhD? There is a big difference!

- What does 'wealthy' mean? $1m or $10m?

- Retire early could be at 63 or 50!

- Get fit could be a walk round the park or a 3:30 marathon

- Beach house could be a shack on the local beach or a 3 storey glass house on an island in the Caribbean!

- Define 'ideal' job: working from home 9-5 or $250k per year in the city?

- "Help people" could be working with the local community or raising $1m for WaterAid

So, if you're going to have goals then work on the SMARTE principles and make them: Specific, Measurable, Attainable, Relevant, Tangible and Exciting. Look at them like this:

- Specific – There should be a number or event in the goal statement, as well as a deadline

- Measurable – I must be able to plot and track my progress towards the goal

- Attainable – It must be something that can be done by me within the timeline set

- Relevant – It must relate to something that is important to me

- Tangible – it must have a real or concrete outcome.

- Exciting – It must 'light a fuse' and be something that gets me excited and energised!

So let's revisit our original dream list and turn them into real SMARTE goals!

- Lose weight – To get from 185 to 155lbs by the 30th August this year and get into that suit that I last wore 5 years ago!

     Live Life Now – Rethink 1440

- Improve qualifications – Enrol part time for the Executive MBA program by 15th September this year and graduate by 20th July 3 years later, so I can apply for my boss's job!

- Be wealthy – To attain a net worth of $2.5m by my 50th birthday and prepare for my two year world travel plan with my family.

- Retire early – To retire from my job at the age of 55 with and unearned/investment income in excess of 80% of my current net salary which has some form of income protection, and to have cleared my home loan by the same date. I'll then be able to start my new business!

- Get fit – To achieve a consistent body mass index of less than 25 and be able to run a 10km race in less than 45 minutes before my 35th Birthday.

- Have a beach house - To purchase for cash, a 2500 square foot property on an 8000 square foot lot with west coast frontage on the island of Grenada in the Caribbean by 31st December 2021, so I can settle down to write my book!

- Get an ideal job - To get a home based sales job that allows me to balance my earning ability at $200k with my family life

- Help others - Sign up with the WaterAid charity and run local events that raise in excess of $25k per year

You see how simple it is to turn dreams into goals? All you have to do next is create a written plan and start working on it. Before you know it you will be healthy, wise and wealthy!

Copy and use the Goal Planning template on the following page and document your top 4 or 5 goals. As you achieve each goal, tick them off, and replace those completed goals with plans for new ones.

The goal planning sheet is split into three main areas:

- Goal – The specific detailed SMARTE goal with a hard deadline
- Benefits – At least one or two compelling reasons why you want to achieve the goal
- Action – A detailed breakdown of the steps you will take to make the goal happen

Plan 2 – Goals

Goal, Benefit, Action Plan

Today's Date _______________ Target Date _____________

Goal

____

____

____

Benefit – The benefits of achieving this goal include:

____

____

____

____

Action – Specific actions I will take to achieve this goal

#1 ____

#2 ____

#3 ____

#4 ____

#5 ____

#6____

#7____

#8 ____

#9 ____

#10 ____

Remember to make your goals SMARTE:
Specific, Measurable, Attainable, Relevant, Tangible
and let them have an Exciting result!

3. Plan to Succeed

Live Life Now – Rethink 1440

"Failures don't plan to fail; they fail to plan!"
Harvey MacKay

There is not a single person who I have spoken to over the years who has not understood the importance of planning, but I estimate that maybe only 20% of them are really good at it. Success is not an accident, or if it is, then lucky you! If you really want success then you need to have a detailed step by step plan for its attainment.

My own personal estimate is that the average person is planning up to a year ahead, but generally only as far as the next major event, which may be a vacation, birthday or other family event. This, in some cases, means that the average planning window may be as little as 3-6 months. Now answer this honestly: "what is your planning window right now?" If you can't identify a specific written goal that is more than 6-12 months in the future, then read on!

A plan to achieve a goal comprises of a series of smaller actions that take you in the direction of the goal. It is not complex. Let's take the weight loss goal from chapter 2 as an example.

Goal
Lose weight – To get from 155 to 135lbs by the 30th August this year.
Benefit
Feel better about myself. Have more energy. Reduce risk of serious illness. Get into that suit I had 5 years ago!
Action

1. Get full medical   15th June
2. Start exercising 3 times per week for 40 mins 20th June
3. List current diet over next 5 days   20th June
4. Meet nutritionist at the gym for new diet   25th June
5. Weigh myself weekly and celebrate!   Weekly
6. Increase exercise to 5 times per week   30th July
7. Put my old suit on!   30th Aug

The simplicity of this process is blindingly simple, so how could you possibly fail? People who aren't hitting their goals are usually guilty of one of the following:

- They don't start – great planners, but equally great procrastinators.
- They don't finish – motivation lapses or they get distracted
- Obstacles get in the way – no consideration for contingencies
- They take on too much – too many goals at the same time
- Goals not SMARTE – impractical and overly optimistic

The bottom line is if you make your goals SMARTE and really build a deep desire for the end 'product' and work with dogged determination, then almost anything is possible!

Spend some time now planning then read on for more guidance!

Plan 3 - Planning

Specific actions I will take to improve my planning:

1. ____

2. ____

3. ____

4. ____

5. ____

Hints: These might include:

- Long term planning 5-10 years out
- Medium term planning 2-3 years out
- Monthly, weekly and daily written plans against specific goals
- Allocating time for each activity
- Prioritising
- Aligning with my dreams!

4. Spend time on the important things

"Life is too short to stuff a mushroom!"
Shirley Conran

Whether you agree with Shirley Conran or not, she has a point! We each have 365 days per year and 24 hours or 1440 minutes per day. It doesn't matter how wealthy or privileged you are, time is the ultimate equalizer. We all have the same amount available every day. Deciding what we do with time is often our biggest challenge. However, it is less challenging if you have clear written goals. The best starting point for prioritising is for each of us to decide what our list of important things look like.

Ask yourself: "What is an 'important thing' to me?" How about something that is taking you in the direction of your goals and also something that matches your values and helps you fulfil your mission or life purpose? You do have a mission, don't you?

When conflicts arise, ask yourself these questions:

- What takes me towards my goals?

- What supports my values and purpose?

- Which item on my list do I really 'want' to do vs. feel like I have to

These questions will help you to prioritise and gain clarity on what's important to you.

Here's an example to help you better understand how to put what we've discussed so far, into practice:

It's Saturday morning and you're well into your regular chores when your son approaches you as you are about to fire up the grass cutter for a couple hours of gardening before heading to the grocery store; "Dad, there's a football match at school I just found out about. Please can you take me and it would be great if you can stay and watch?" What do you do? The grass needs cutting, the refrigerator is almost empty, you are heading for a 'best kept garden' prize in a couple of weeks and Ricky forgot to tell you about a football game. This is a classic example of goal vs. purpose and mission.

- *Goal – win a gardening prize this year*

- *Mission – to be a great father to my kids*

What would you do? Easy eh! Take Ricky to the football match, skip the shopping trip and cut the lawn later before it gets dark; then find an 'open all hours' store later at night to take care of the grocery essentials. Sure your planned Saturday routine got messed up but the important things got done, in the right order!

This is yet another great reason to have goals and to understand your purpose. It helps you to prioritise and spend your time doing the 'right' things.

Your next prioritising goal is to balance your time while looking at your 'important things' list and freeing up time from your 1440 allocation. Inevitably this means a shift in the activities that you do. My favourite and most effective way to do this is to create a Stop, Start, and Continue (SSC) list. There are things you need to stop or limit doing, new things you need to start doing and finally continue doing those things you're already doing that take you towards your goals.

Stop List

If you are doing things that are not important, that are not taking you towards your goals then stop doing them or limit the time allocated to acting on them. I frequently ask people what their primary challenge is in getting to the gym, reading, getting new qualifications, spending time with their families etc. I get the same types of answers and it is usually along the lines of "I don't have the time". Then I ask the magic question: "How much TV do you watch"? More than 90% of the people I ask watch 4 hours or more of TV per day. Generally the results shock them. A recent study in 2017 found that the average American watches 5 hours of TV per day. That is 35 hours per week of couch potato time. Examine how TV-watching time negatively affects your potentials: mental, physical, emotional and spiritual/ethical.

I am not advocating zero TV by the way, just look at your priorities and work on balance. So maybe you 'Stop' actions might be

- Stop watching TV
  - Completely for three days a week
  - After 9pm rest of the week
- Benefit
  - 15 hours per week spent on studying for my MBA
  - 5 hours per week working with my kids on their homework

Start List

So you've now freed up plenty of time to start doing some new things that take you towards your goals and you are motivated to change. Now it's time to draw up your 'start' list.

Examples:
- Four 40 minute cardio sessions per week
- Reduce junk food intake by 50%
- Sign up for flying lessons
- Open savings account for new home
- Investigate new business opportunities

Continue List

There are going to be a whole series of things you are already doing, but it's still a great idea to list them so you keep your focus!

Examples
- Working hard on next career move
- Spending time with my family
- Studying for my MBA

Plan 4 - Priorities

Things that will help me define the 'right' things:

My mission or purpose is:

____
____
____
____
____
____
____

These are most important to me right now:
(e.g. family, career, friends, finances, health, spirituality)

1. ____
   ____
2. ____
   ____
3. ____
   ____
4. ____
   ____
5. ____
   ____

My personal SSC list

	Activity	Benefit
Stop		
Start		
Continue		

5. Start now

I'm making a list of
some things I ought to do...
I'm calling it my
"ought-to-biography!"
LIFE LIST
AEROBI_

"What is not started today is never finished tomorrow"
Goethe

Or, put another way, "Never put off until tomorrow what you can do today, because, if you do it today and like it, you can do it again tomorrow!" Procrastination is at the heart of failure to achieve goals. I have met some amazing goal setters who have documented page after page of plans for their short, medium and long term achievements, but are stuck, making no progress. They simply haven't begun to implement any of their plans! Why on earth would you go through the process of planning your goals and never start acting on them? Or, worse still, get started and then stop. The reasons maybe amongst these:

- Fear of failure – worried that you might be pushing yourself too far
- Analysis paralysis – overly concerned with the details
- Not motivated – a lack of 'fire in the belly'
- Too 'busy' – other things getting in your way
- Overwhelmed - by the sheer size of your goal
- Not my goal – someone else set it for me

If you are suffering because of any of the reasons identified then now is the time to take action. Choose accordingly from the following list:

- Fear of failure – build confidence in your ability to achieve the goal. Break it into smaller easier goals. Celebrate small victories.

- Analysis paralysis - Work out how to do 'just enough' planning, with 'just enough' information and 'just enough' resources. Retired US Secretary of State, Colin Powell, came up with the 40-70% principle which can be applied in these circumstances. He reckons that 40% of all available information is the minimum required to make a decision and 70% is the most. If you have less than 40% then get more. If you have 70% or close then stop looking. Make the decision and start based on the facts you have and leave the rest to your 'gut' or experience!

- Not motivated – figure out why you want to achieve the results once you achieve the goal. Work out what is in it for you. If you can't answer three or four 'why' questions about the goal, or write down a couple of major reasons as to what you will experience as a result then don't bother with it and find something more exciting to work on!

- Too 'busy' – if you really are too busy and it's not a cop out, then, you either have too many goals, or you haven't planned effectively. Go back and reprioritise your wants and settle on the top four or five most important goals, then plan and schedule the time to work on each goal.

- Overwhelmed – break the goal down to small pieces

- Not my goal – if someone else set the goal for you then you need to ask the question: "does it align with my purpose, values or mission and is it something that I want?" If the answer is to either question is 'no' then you need to consider whether to take action on the goal. Be careful if the goal is being set by your boss though!

Never forget – 'Good things come to those who wait, but only the things left behind by those who set goals and hustle. Let's hustle!'

Plan 5 – Overcoming Obstacles

Ask yourself, "what holds me back in the pursuit of my goals?" For example if it is finding time, then plan and schedule small time slots every day for the new activity and stop doing things that have little value.

These are the things that hold me back and the actions I will take to get started!

What holds me back?	My action to overcome

6. Don't be afraid!

One of the greatest reasons we put off doing things differently, or starting new goals, is the fear of failure or the fear of something that we have to do to achieve the goal. Fear itself can also hold us back from setting change and achievement goals in the first place. So being afraid can be a major hold back on our progress to achieving our potentials and our monster goals. There is absolutely nothing wrong with being afraid and having 'fears'. It's human nature. The difference between those who achieve greatness and those who languish in mediocrity is not so much their fears, but how they choose to see those fears. "There is nothing to fear but fear itself", sums it up.

Imagine where we would be if:

- Columbus had succumbed to his fear of sailing off the edge of the world
- Edison was dissuaded by the number of times he failed to find the right filament for the electric light bulb
- The Wright brothers had worries about crashing their first aeroplane
- Sir Richard Branson got a regular job because he feared for his financial security
- Beyoncé suffered from stage fright at her first concert

Quite simply, you hold yourself back from reaching your dreams by succumbing to your fears. My analytical mind and past-life career as an engineer encouraged me to represent the process as an easy to remember formula or equation.

$$R = G - SD^2$$

Where;

R = Results
G = Goals
SD^2 = Self Doubt squared!

So a small amount of self-doubt is going to be a massive hold back on the achievement of your goals. Remove all self-doubt by squashing your fears and you will achieve all that you set out to do!

I have seen, heard and experienced using some great tactics in overcoming fears. Let me share some:

- Take a look at why the fear exists. We are conditioned people. In other words we have learned from our environment, especially the people around us. Experiences also condition us, so somewhere in our past lies the clues to our present behaviour. Don't allow past experience to influence your future! If you are scared of dogs maybe you got a dog bite as a child. If you are risk averse it's possible that your parents may have also been that way, or perhaps an early business venture of yours may have failed. Knowing why the fear is there is a small step towards minimising or removing it completely

- Take small steps. Let's imagine you are afraid of water, but you want to learn to swim. Jumping in the deep end of the pool is one approach, but it may not cure your fear. Follow how I approached curing my own fear of swimming in December 2010:
  1. I set goals that involved swimming: swim with dolphins and manta rays and complete a triathlon (swimming, cycling and running the race).
  2. I got in the shallow end of a pool. Breathed in, bobbed my face under water then breathed out through my nose and mouth. I repeated this until it felt natural. I did the same, but in the deep end holding onto the side. Again, until I was comfortable.
  3. I celebrated my small victory
  4. Signed up for swimming lessons
  5. Practiced and trained regularly

- Complete your goals. I completed my first triathlon on the 28th May 2011, my first Ironman triathlon on the 1st Dec 2013 and now hold an Advanced PADI scuba diving card. I have already swum in the company of a manta ray in Trinidad, dived with sharks on a reef in the Bahamas and plan to share some sea time with dolphins very soon.

- Attack them head on. A more radical approach is to simply face your fears head on, growl at them, and attack! It may seem odd for someone who is afraid of heights to become a pilot, but being in that cocoon of a cockpit was comfortable, I could look out from a height of several thousand feet while up in the air, and not be bothered, but weirdly, if I looked off the balcony of a tenth floor hotel room my stomach churned and I would feel dizzy. So my paragliding goal kept looking like a real tough one. I finally decided, attack this head on. The day before my 60th Birthday I signed up with 30 minutes notice to do a paraglide flight way up in the northern Andes in Colombia. It was a snap decision and before I knew it I was suited up and pilot Alejandro tapped my shoulder and we stepped off a 10,000ft cliff! After the first 10-15 seconds of abject fear I had the most amazing 20 minutes of flight. I'll be back and I'm going to sign up to do solo flights next year!

- Talk yourself out of it. Affirmations are a powerful tool to help you rid yourself of your fears. Remember that we all talk to ourselves. An affirmation is just another form of that, directed at overcoming our fears. During my early swimming endeavours I proclaimed myself to be "a swimming monster!" I did it loudly and sometimes in public. It was so effective that others in my beginner's class also adopted the affirmation! Of course it wasn't true at the time since I could barely get from one side of the kid pool to the other, but the constant repetition of this one affirmation, in my head helped drive me to work harder and harder and build my confidence so today when I say it, it is the truth: "I am indeed a swimming monster!"

- Visualise the result. All great goal achievers excel at visualizing the end result. I used to fear public speaking. I knew that if I wanted to achieve my ambitions to positively change the lives of thousands of people in my lifetime, I wouldn't achieve that goal talking to one person at a time; it would mean slow progress, so I threw that out as an option Instead, I cut out a huge crowd image from a big event photo that I found on the internet and cut and pasted an image of myself onto that stage. I scanned the final image and used it as my PC wallpaper for months as I did presentations to more and more people. The image was always in my head as I walked onto the stage. Now the more people I speak to the better I feel. That fear is still there, especially during the first 2-3 minutes, but nobody knows about it but me and it doesn't prevent me from going on stage to positively change the lives of others. Bring on the 500+ crowds!

- Avoid naysayers and hang out with positive people or people who are on the same journey as you. This has the effect of increasing your confidence as well as learning new ways to achieve your goals.

- Read, learn and do whatever it takes to build your skills in alignment with the new world you want to grow towards. If you are going to leave your job and start a new business, find on-line resources to help you. Go watch YouTube videos, listen to podcasts and read real books to help!

So fear is to be celebrated, welcomed and then attacked with vigour and confidence!

Plan 6 – Don't be afraid

Fear and approach:

Fear	Approach	Affirmation

Hints:
Fear: Financial insecurity/risk – but want to start own business
Approach: Open a savings account. Do detailed risk analysis of your venture. Write down a list of the worst that could happen and the best that <u>will</u> happen. Find positive people to support you. Then start!
Affirmation: I am a profitable business owner!

7. Don't think outside the box

You must have heard that tired old cliché encouraging you to "Think outside the box", challenging you to look at things differently. Well, how about changing that to "Don't think outside the box; imagine there was never a box in the first place!". It is true that if you want to achieve extraordinary things then you have to think in radical ways. Conventional thinkers look at different ways to solve problems, come up with new ideas based on what they know already, or by researching what others know or have done. That is not radical thinking! Although it may be termed thinking outside the box in its most extreme form.

The real radical thinkers achieve extraordinary results by clearing their minds of previous conditioning and getting themselves into a state where boxes can never exist! In this state they are free to truly be creative. The older we get the more conditioned we become and the more challenging it is to be truly creative. Although we may have the experience and intellect, we are all fundamentally boxed in.

Some great innovators and business leaders had little formal education when they made major breakthroughs and one could say that there is a great benefit to that. How so? Well, a conventional education can lead to conventional thinking. Undisciplined creative thinking, brought about by a less conventional upbringing and education, sometimes is the key to more radical breakthroughs and innovation. Think about these examples:

- Physicist, Albert Einstein famously got bad marks in his early education and flunked conventional school. He fought against what he termed 'rote' learning and the effect it had on creative thought. He went on to become one of the most radical thinkers of the 20th century and today is considered the father of modern physics.

- Thomas Edison was a prolific inventor and brought us recorded sound and the light bulb. Edison spent just three months in conventional school where he could not concentrate and was described as 'addled' in his thinking. He was then home taught and left to learn at his own pace and study those things that interested him. He was a compulsive reader and experimenter.

- Founder of the Ford Motor Company, Henry Ford, with just 8 years of conventional schooling in a small one room school, broke pretty much every conventional 'rule' in the early 20th century manufacturing sector. He challenged traditional thinking and radically transformed the automotive industry with the first ever moving production line and mass part manufacturing, which enabled him to produce low cost transportation which transformed much of American life.

- Billionaire and head of the Virgin Group, Sir Richard Branson, left school with a poor academic record at 17 and went on to become one of the most creative entrepreneurs of our time. He constantly challenges convention and seeks out brand new ways of doing things. He built his Virgin brand as a global empire with some 360 companies.

However you choose to tap into your unconventional side, be it through meditation, attending retreats, facilitation, or re-education, if you want to totally transform your life, or just push the 'better button' don't forget - being creative keeps you young and helps you get what you want.

Plan 7 – Creative thinking

Specific actions I will take to work on my creativity:

1. ____

   ____

2. ____

   ____

3. ____

   ____

4. ____

   ____

5. ____

   ____

Hints : These might include:
- Plan a short retreat for myself
- Spend some time every week 'thinking'
- Hang around with creative people
- Question using 'why'
- Get up an hour earlier in the morning to reflect and meditate

8. Life balance is personal

*"I never recall anyone saying on their death bed that they wished
they'd spent more time at the office"*
Anon – Doctor

Interesting comment, but don't ever assume that everyone is like you! I have met some very successful business people who genuinely choose to work long, long hours despite the fact that they don't need the money, or any other substantial material gain from their labours. Why do they do it then when they could be: playing golf, being with friends and family, working out and so on? The short answer? There is something that they like to do at 'work' better than those other choices. But one thing you can be sure of is that everyone's view of balancing these choices will be different.

Let's get straight about one of my personal dislikes: the term 'work/life balance'. What's wrong with that? In my view, the implication is that there is 'work' and 'life' and somehow the two aren't linked; that work is not life. This probably comes from the idea that work is somehow unpleasant and not 'life', and that real 'life' starts when 'work' ends. Using the term reinforces the message that work and life are somehow separate. In fact they are one and the same, and work is part of most people's lives, so why not make the most of it!

If balance is personal, how do we then control what we do and how much time we spend doing 'it'? Goals and values will certainly be influencing factors and will determine a great deal about how you spend your time, but in order to figure out our own personal version of balance, it might be a good idea to look at your choices today and then decide what you may want to change in the future. You might want to consider the varying activities in your life and how they fit into these categories:

- Head – mental development, education
- Need – financial, security, environment
- Heart – contentment, love, joy, spirituality
- Belonging – family, friends, social
- Body – diet, fitness, health

Don't forget those around you when you are working out what balance looks like in your life. Examine everyone and everything.

There is an even easier way to get balance and that is to make work so enjoyable that it doesn't feel like work, because if you do what you love, you will never have to work another day in your life.

In the Action plan that follows evaluate your satisfaction with your current 'balance' and see where you want things to be in the future. Who knows, more goals may follow!

Plan 8 – Balancing life

In the table below rate each of the 5 major areas of your life. Think about how satisfied you are with that area. Now rate yourself below, where 0 = very dissatisfied and 10 being very satisfied. Once you have those scores then think 2-3 years into the future and give yourself a second rating based on where you would like to be. Now take one from the other and you will have identified your 'gap' i.e. the difference between where you stand today and your ideal in the future. This should give you a clear set of priorities.

	Area	Now 0-10	Future 0-10.	Gap	Priority 1-5.
1	**Head:** mental development, education, learning, intellect				
2	**Need:** financial, security, environment				
3	**Heart:** contentment, love, joy, spirituality				
4	**Belonging:** family, friends, social, cultural				
5	**Body:** diet, fitness, health, lifestyle				

Top Balance Priorities:

1. ____
2. ____
3. ____
4. ____
5. ____

Specific actions I will take to improve my life balance:

1. ____

   ____

   ____

2. ____

   ____

   ____

3. ____

   ____

   ____

4. ____

   ____

   ____

5. ____

   ____

   ____

Hints: these might include:

- Develop a career plan
- Spend an hour every day with my son/daughter on their homework
- Join a gym and do a daily workout
- Watch on-line videos on business development

9. You won't get what you want without help

You will always 'get by' in life but it's infinitely better when you have some help and support. On this exciting journey through life we all need the support of people around us, but this should not go in one direction. We should also create balance by being the providers of support to others where possible. There is in fact, a great philosophy which suggests that if you take on the role of a servant, and spend a proportion of your time helping others, then you will get back your time investment many times over. I'm not sure there is quantitative evidence to support this but it does sound like a solid piece of advice. Certainly the 'users' in our society - those who take, take, take will eventually get what is coming to them!

So to achieve our goals and objectives, where can we look for support and assistance? Look at every one of your goals and objectives and have a clear view as to who can help, and especially look at how they will benefit in the process of helping you succeed. (See more on this in the accompanying plan of action.)

Take a look at these activities and look at the magnitude of the 'help' needed in order to achieve your goals:

- Get an MBA – Your coach, lecturers, book authors, supporters and family
- Publish a book – At least 10 people plus the author including reviewers, editor, print advisor, cover and graphic designer, and printer.
- Run a marathon - start officials, marshals, race supporters and the people to hand you your medal at the end!

This just touches the tip of the iceberg though because more often than not the real 'help' that you get from your friends and people around you is less tangible. En route to success there are basically three types of people:

1. those who will support you
2. those who are neutral and
3. those who well, to put it bluntly, get in your way

When people 'get in your way' it may not always be in a physical sense. Usually they get in your way by questioning your attitude and self-beliefs. They often see themselves as well-meaning and are always ready to dispense advice especially when you share your goals with them, particularly your big goals!

"Setting up your own business, isn't that risky in this environment?"

"A marathon! That's a long way for someone your age, you should see a doctor. I heard that someone died last year doing that!"

"Why do you need a bigger house? We were brought up in a house smaller than the one you are in now and it was good enough for us..."

"Flying lessons! Now that's just plain crazy at this time in your life. Did you see that documentary on the frequency of air accidents the other day?"

Any of these sound familiar?

One I heard when I was talking about learning to swim "at your age, you must be crazy you'll never learn at your time of life"!

The last thing you need at a time when you are planning and taking action on your goals are friends like that. The people who can really help are those that support you with encouraging words and a positive attitude; those that help you build your confidence up rather than tear it down. It is a great idea to make a list of your friends and family members then categorise them into three areas:

1. Supporters – they will cheer and yell when you announce your latest goal, celebrate your successes on the way, and even emulate some of your behaviours. When you have challenges

they will be there to support and guide. Spend as much time as you can with these people!

2. Neutral – neither one thing nor the other. They will probably just nod sagely when they hear about your goals and adventures. Work with them to show them the benefits of what you are doing and maybe you'll get some positive converts!

3. Naysayers – they doubt what you do, make negative comments to your face and to your friends and may even question your levels of responsibility and even your sanity. Avoid people in this group at all costs!

I remember the day I declared that I was going to sail across the Atlantic. There were definitely two camps of people: those who supported and the naysayers. The naysayers came at me with: "you have to be crazy, it's still the hurricane season", "did you know I heard that a boat was lost with its crew in that race last year". The comments from my supporters far outweighed the unsupportive comments of the naysayers: "yeah, great Nigel! Send us messages", "what is the tracking link? We want to see what you're doing every step of the way!".

I've been sailing for more years than I care to remember, but this marked the first trip working with crew. I realised just hours into the crossing in crazy winds and seas off the African coast how absolutely dependent we were on each other. One false move from a fellow crew member would have repercussions for all on board.

That level of interdependence was very new to me and uncomfortable at first. As time progressed and we managed the boat through the worst of the weather I became more comfortable placing my trust in my fellow crew mates. I learned a great lesson and by the time we finished the 21 day crossing, docking in St Lucia, I realised just how important having support is as you work towards your goals!

So surround yourself with positive people, hang out with other successful people and avoid the naysayers; give more than you take and when you do need support, you will have plenty of people there to help you!

Plan 9 – Getting help

Who can help me and what can I do for them:

What help do I need?	Supporter.	What's in it for them?

Hints:

For example - Steven is a supporter in my quest to run a marathon. He can help get me a training schedule. He hates to train alone so we can run together.

10. Don't bet your future on luck

"The safest way to double your money is to fold it over once and put it back in your pocket."
Kin Hubbard

Did you know that the chances of winning a 'fortune' in a national or state lottery are very, very, very small. Bear with me while I demonstrate using a national lottery example, which can be won with six numbers in the range 1 to 49. A typical jackpot win in the lottery would be around US$3 million. Six numbers are drawn at random from the set of integers between 1 and 49, which means there are 49!/(6!*(49-6)!) combinations of numbers (the draw order doesn't matter). '!' is the mathematical term for 'factorial', so 49! is 49*48*47*46 and so on. This means that the jackpot chance is 1 in 13,983,816 or approximately 1 in 14 million. So if you bet $14 million you can be pretty sure to get $3 million back. Not a great deal eh?

The old gambler's retort to this type of logic is typically "well someone has to win and it could be me!" Yes, I have to agree and if you are OK with odds of 14 million to 1 then don't let me hold you back from investing your hard-earned money in lottery tickets! You are five times more likely to be struck by lightning though so take care on thundery days!

The main question is: are you prepared to bet your future success on the turn of a card, the roll of the dice or the odds of the lottery machine? If not, then now is the time to plan with certainty knowing that through goal setting, planning and high activity you are going to be far more successful in getting what you want, when you want it.

The serious point to consider is this: It's not just gamblers betting on success. Most of us do it on a day to day basis without realising it. Ask yourself the following:

- How much of my day is truly mine?
- How many decisions are mine?
- Who is in control?

- Who am I dependent on?
- Who besides me, weighs in on those crucial decisions in my life?

Determine how much of your life today is controlled by you and how much is based on the decisions of others. If someone else is controlling your life then your success will be based largely on luck. So when we say 'don't bet your future on luck' we really mean 'take control and make your own decisions', because in a bet, there is a fool and a thief.

Plan 10 – My decisions

Decisions that only I can make:

Decision	Outcome	When

For example:

Decision: Where shall I do my Law Degree?

Outcome: University of London

Date: 9th September 2025

 Live Life Now – Rethink 1440

11. How to eat an Elephant

"Whoever wants to reach a distant goal must take many small steps!"
Helmut Schmidt

And that's how to eat an elephant- "one bite at a time".

When you look at your dream list and the goals that have come out of them, start thinking about categorising them; maybe according to easy, medium and tough; or small, medium and large. The easy and small goals are likely to be ones you can list and action without any great pain or challenge.

- Lose 10lbs in the next two months by watching my diet and working out three times a week
- Read two business books in the next two months as groundwork for the start of my MBA program in June

These are hardly elephant-sized goals and shouldn't be too challenging; just a matter of scheduling the time and motivating and energising yourself into action.

What do the real elephant-sized goals look like? Well, they are likely to be the longer term goals that require a more substantial shift in behaviour, financing, attitude and maybe even higher risk.

The process for hitting these big goals is relatively simple and I will outline the process first before showing real life examples that will demonstrate its simplicity and prove that it really does work.

- Take the elephant goal and subdivide it into 3-5 smaller goals
- Put these goals in time sequence
- Work out what, if anything, can be done in parallel
- Document the smaller goals using the process shown in chapter three
- See if there are any small elephants in your new goal list. If so break them down until all of the goals you have are relatively 'easy'.

Do not underestimate it because it's simple. The fact remains - it works! Let's take a look at this example: if I said my goal was to read 10-15 business books in a year that may sound like an elephant goal. However if I broke it down and set a goal to read just 10 pages of a book for 30 minutes every day I'd achieve my goal of reading 10 to 15 books a year but my process (reading just 10 pages for 30 minutes a day) makes it possible because it's an easy action to take.

Let me illustrate by using real life examples of my own elephants and how I "ate them, one bite at a time."

Elephant #1 - To run all of the Comrades 90km Ultra Marathon in South Africa in June 2007 in under 10 hours. Set in 2004.

For background, when I set this goal I had only ever run half marathons at 13.1 miles and was in the process of training for my first full marathon at 26.2 miles. The Comrades Ultra Marathon is 56 miles (90km) and added to that, it is in the hills of KwaZulu-Natal in South Africa and has to be completed in under 12 hours. I had never run on serious hills before so it was over four times the distance I was used to, and due to work and other race commitments, I could only train for six months prior to the race. Also, there was the simple logistics of getting there from the Caribbean with a very short window of opportunity in-between other major work commitments. This was indeed an elephant!

Sub Goals
- Lose 20 lbs in 10 weeks from January to mid-March 2007 by:
  - Focussed sports nutrition plan
  - Zero alcohol
  - Increase in easy running mileage
  - Low intensity core exercises
- Increase running mileage from 30 miles per week in January to peak at 100 miles per week for 2 weeks in May
  - Run every day, even if just 5 miles
  - Plan long runs every other Sunday up to 30 miles
  - Plan work trips to be in areas where I can still run

- Cut back on non-essential personal expenses to save the US$7,500 total trip cost
  - Put off new bike purchase
  - Fit in a business meeting while travelling
  - Visit family on the way to get other goals on the trip
- Reassign one work project to a colleague to allow me to take the time off
  - Introduce colleague to client
  - Train colleague on the project
  - Do dry runs to ensure project success

So my big elephant was split into four smaller goals, of which one was a small elephant i.e. building the mileage from 30 to over 100. Even I was overwhelmed by that to start with and I had to work it down to a weekly plan where I just added a few miles and an extra run, then celebrated the progress. I took an easier week then back up again until, as if by magic, I looked at my training plan in mid-May to find I had run 102 miles in a single week without any sign of injury.

Needless to say I completed the Ultra Marathon and beat my 10 hour goal by just over 20 minutes, finishing in 9 hours 39 minutes and 52 seconds. I enjoyed it so much I went back in 2008 and did it again, this time in reverse; it was no longer an elephant!

Elephant #2 - To write and have published a 'bestselling' Leadership book by end of December 2008. Set in Dec 2006.

The context for this is that I had always wanted to write a book on leadership, but hadn't started. At the time I wrote the goal, two years looked straightforward, but I was to learn that this particular elephant had a bit of a kick in its tail. I had only a few minor articles published in local and regional papers and business magazines, so this was also a big elephant!

Sub Goals

- Determine subject and create outline
    - Research gaps in leadership publications
    - Discuss with clients
    - Test market concepts
    - Write key headers
- Build content
    - Determine key times for the creative input (given that I have busy days coaching)
        - One hour 06:30 to 07:30 each morning
        - Use 'dead' times between client meetings. Especially in the mornings
    - Buy a lightweight laptop with long battery life
    - Set weekly word count goals
- Review and Publish
    - Identify possible reviewers
    - Send regular drafts to reviewers
    - Identify possible publishers
    - Send drafts and reviewed manuscripts to publishers
- Launch and Market
    - Identify key routes to market
    - Identify global network
    - Ensure book gets to internet network via Amazon

Can you identify the smaller elephant on my sub-goal list? That's right - finding a publisher! It was a huge project that required thick skin, some creative work and especially, dogged determination. The detailed plan to get the book published was almost as big as the overall plan for the rest of the book, but by breaking it down into bite-sized chunks the elephant finally got eaten! The book, Ask Leadership, was launched on the 18th November 2008, 42 days before the goal deadline by an international publisher, who had it on amazon.com on the day of the launch.

So, taking that elephant goal and breaking it down into smaller 'edible' pieces was the secret to achieving the biggest of all goals.

Ask yourself this: "which piece of the elephant did I eat today?"

Plan 11 - Elephants

My Elephant Goals:

Elephant Goal	Sub Goals
	1 _________________________ 2 _________________________ 3 _________________________ 4 _________________________ 5 _________________________
	1 _________________________ 2 _________________________ 3 _________________________ 4 _________________________ 5 _________________________
	1 _________________________ 2 _________________________ 3 _________________________ 4 _________________________ 5 _________________________
	1 _________________________ 2 _________________________ 3 _________________________ 4 _________________________ 5 _________________________
	1 _________________________ 2 _________________________ 3 _________________________ 4 _________________________ 5 _________________________

12. Make Choices

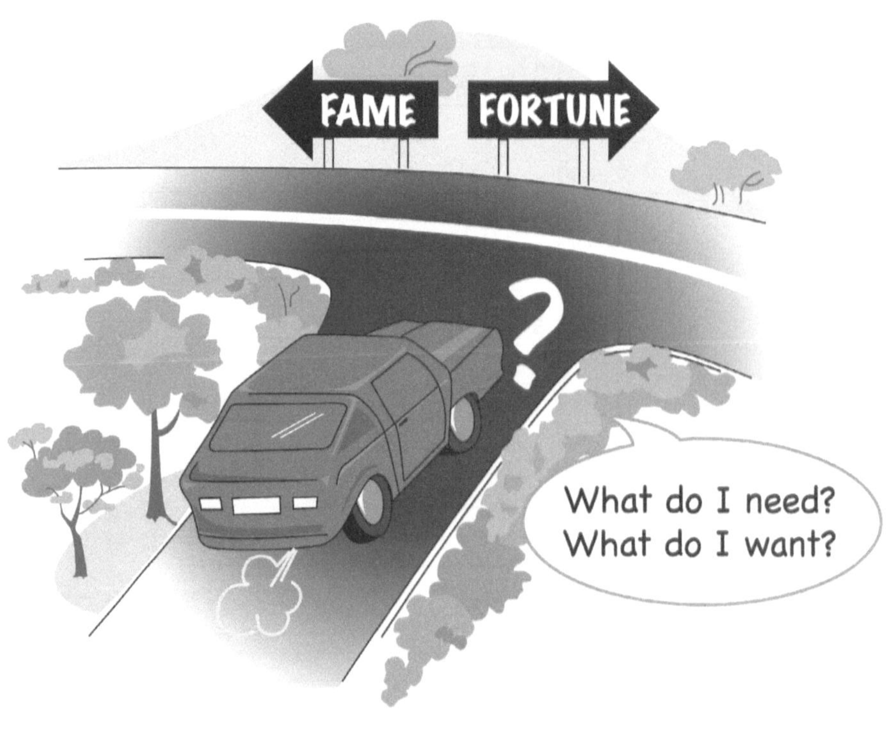

"There are two primary choices in life; to accept conditions as they exist, or accept the responsibility for changing them"
Denis Waitley

Actually there is a third choice and that is to get out of the conditions you dislike by moving on! All are equally valid as long as you accept personal responsibility for all your choices. If you fail to make choices yourself then someone else will, either directly or indirectly, and you will wind up in a place you don't want to be, and guess who's to blame? If you are not sure of the answer then go look in a mirror!

So look at these three choices and get very focussed, especially if you are unhappy with your current situation.

Choice #1 – Learn to live with things as they are

Choice #2 – Work hard to positively change things

Choice #3 – Leave

Note the lack of a fourth choice to moan, whine and complain. It does not exist. If you make clear choices then you have no need to be negative and complain. The added stress and negative effect will be debilitating to you and others. You will feel better about yourself and the world around you when you take control and 'decide'.

I have conversations with many of my 'students', and when they declare their unhappiness in a particular aspect of their life, I challenge them with the three choices. Few are happy with choice #1 and most are uncomfortable with choice #3, so the biggest focus is attacking the problem head on and working on positive change. Those that have the highest success rate are those who take personal responsibility for making the changes happen and do not blame external circumstances or other people.

There are some bold people who get to such a level of dissatisfaction or unhappiness that they do choose to leave and restart. It could be a relationship, job, social circle or even country! I have been there in a couple of situations. The most significant change I made in 2001 was to quit the IT industry and to start my own business as a leadership coach, author and speaker. I had worked for over 20 years in the industry and it moved from a 'love' to 'dislike' relationship. The industry became more competitive and there were frequent 'downsizing' episodes with increased stress! In the past I had tried choices #1 and #2 without success. It was time for a bold move - choice #3!

I left my last job with just six months of savings in the bank to pay my mortgage, and all the other household bills. I spent those six months learning the new skills required and networking for potential clients. In month five I had some great contacts and materials from a franchise. In month six I got my first batch of clients, and the rest, as they say is history. Sometime you have to jump off the cliff and build your wings on the way down!

So choice is not just about life decisions, it's also about your attitude and how you approach things. More of this later!

Plan 12 – Confidence builders

Specific actions I will take to build my confidence and make my own choices:

1. ____

____

2. ____

____

3. ____

____

4. ____

____

5. ____

____

____

Hints: These might include:
- Learn to say 'no' without hurting too many feelings
- Recognise and be aware of when I do have a choice
- Stand up for my own beliefs
- Stop complaining when I don't like my environment and take action to improve things or leave

13. Look after yourself

As we have already noted, the average person uses a small, and I mean very small, percentage of their physical potential. Not only that, but there has recently been a massive increase in the rates of obesity and the consequences of that which include: heart disease, stroke, diabetes, some cancers, breathing problems and many others. To put things more bluntly: which of the following appeals to you most?

A. Wealthy, overweight, inactive and heading for an early grave
B. Healthy, wealthy and wise

No-brainer really, isn't it? And the choice really is yours. There are also two ways to look at the prospect of building your health:

1. It is a necessary evil and you must do it
2. It is a great experience and the end results are well worth every ounce of energy and determination you put into it

If your head is in #1, then the diet and trips to the gym will be seen as just another thing that you 'have' to do. You will also probably not stick to it for long and lapse into your old ways. Attitude #2 is the one that will produce long-term sustainable results and also have you enjoying your new-found youth.

Let's kick this session off by dispelling some myths and getting down to the basics of looking after yourself.

Myth vs. reality

- "I have a weight problem." No, you have an 'attitude towards yourself' problem and some bad habits!
- "Obesity runs in our family." It may do, but it's not hereditary. What runs in your family are poor eating and lifestyle habits.

- "What I eat determines my weight." Not always. There is a direct link between weight gain and activity level. Inactivity is a major cause of weight gain and obesity in most developed countries.

Changing Life

Whether you are clinically obese or just plain overweight and not exercising, the first thing you need to fix is your attitude, and especially your attitude towards yourself. The good news is that this is a simple process. And guess what? It uses a principle that you already know about, goal-setting. Yes, it's all about goals. Remember, to change past conditioning requires you to repeatedly do things differently. When you've done them 20-30 times, they become your new habits and you will have, in the process, successfully displaced the old ones.

In order to start the change process you first need to ask why and then keep asking why until you have at least five or six great reasons to change. Ask yourself the following:

- What is my goal?
- Why do I want to achieve it?
- What will the result look like?
- Why is it important to me?
- Do I have a burning desire to change?
- Am I prepared to put in the time and effort to achieve it?
- Who do I need to share it with?
- Who can support me?

When, and only when, you can really look in the mirror and convince yourself you have satisfied all of these, do you move to the next stage. Let me give you a personal example of when I started a major personal transformation in my early forties.

- The Goal - To be fitter at the age of 50 than at any time in my past. This would be measured by completing a major endurance event (greater than 5 hours) on or before my 50th birthday. At the time I set the goal I was a smoker, 50 pounds overweight and did little to no exercise.

     Live Life Now – Rethink 1440

- Why? The doctor was not impressed at my last medical and suggested that getting to 50 without suffering an 'event' might be unlikely.
- What will the result look like? Fit, energised, looking good, less colds and flu, no coughing.
- Why is it important to me? I want to see my daughters finish college, get married and be fit enough to see them well into middle age. I also really wanted to be a Grandfather!
- Do I have a burning desire to change? Yes!
- Am I prepared to put in the time and effort to achieve it? Yes!
- Who do I need to share it with? My partner and close friends.
- Who can support me? My family and close friends.

Two days before my 50th birthday I completed one of the toughest multi-sport endurance races in the world with a very respectable 11th placing. Goal achieved!

It didn't stop there though, because health and fitness is an ongoing set of activities and attitudes. Despite my success I had got the bug and I went on to confound myself and those around me by completing;

- Nine Half Marathons Personal Best (PB) time 1:45
- Five Full Marathons PB 3:51
- Four ultra-marathons of 56 miles PB 9:39
- Three two-day multisport races trail run, ride and kayak - best 11th out of 35
- Eight Sprint Triathlons PB 1:21
- Five Olympic Triathlons PB 2:49
- Half Ironman Triathlon PB 6:41
- Ironman Triathlon PB 12:54
- 300 mile cycle ride in 23:11
- 101 mile run on my 59th birthday in 29 hours

You don't have to do what I do, but you could!

I have outlined some simple actions below that will help get you back in control and increase the odds of you living a longer and happier life.

Exercise Tips

For now though it's back to basics and time to get yourself into your version of 'fit'. Given that low levels of activity contribute to weight gain and/or obesity it is a good idea to start with that. Here are some guidelines on building activity levels. We can start easy and then build to a more structured approach.

1. Make sure you have clear goals.

    They might be something like: to lose 15 pounds and maintain a body weight of 165 pounds within the next three months. To get my waist size back to 32in and be able to run continuously for 30 minutes within that period. These three goals are actually all linked.

2. Start easy and celebrate each success.

    During the day walk whenever you can: use stairs rather than elevators, park at the furthest end of the car park, walk to the store round the corner rather than drive and so on. Walk the dog for 30 minutes every morning before heading to work. When walking, walk briskly.

3. Moving up a notch

    To really build your fitness and hit your goals, it is important to do something that you like to do. This will be determined by your environment, where you live and the available time you make for yourself. Also consider whether you would be better motivated by working out on your own or in a group. You might pick from these and they are listed in order of burn rate per hour i.e. how effective they are in burning calories:

    a. Running – Treadmill or outdoor 700-1000 calories
    b. Cycling – Spinning or outdoor 500-700 calories

    c.   Swimming - 400-600 calories

You may also consider aerobics classes or a home on-line program to work out to. If you are able, mix two or three of the above to add variety to your workouts. If you do all three you may find yourself at a triathlon some time in your future!

4.   Time and intensity

A minimum of 3 days at 30 minutes per day at each workout (with added warm up and cool down of say 10-15 minutes) will get you moving and have a noticeable effect on your fitness and weight over time, as long as you get into the zone of aerobic exercise. There are many technical ways to calculate when you are in this zone and often, gym equipment will help you out with heart rates. A simpler way to tell if you are in the zone is that you will be working at a rate that will just allow you to have a conversation with a real, or imagined, training partner. If you are so breathless that this is not possible then back off a little. If it's too easy then move the pace up.

Realistically if you want to get really fit, trim and energised then the more you work out the better the end result. People will talk about the possibilities of injury and sure, you should get a medical before you start, especially if you are coming from a base of a very low-fitness level and/or illness. The bottom line is that since you are probably using only a small percentage of your physical potential right now, you can achieve huge levels of fitness in a relatively short period of time.

In Chapter 15 you will read about a couple of real 'mature' fit people, so if you are considering your age as a possible drawback, prepare to be inspired!

Nutrition

If you do nothing other than increase your activity levels you will look and feel better, but if you deal with getting a balanced diet then you will more than double your payback. I have a personal dislike for the way the word 'diet' is used, and also how it is perceived. Generally people see 'diet' as a relatively short-term fix to a weight problem. It is also fair to say that it is not usually seen as a positive activity by those who need it. So let's redefine the word and the concept. My least favourite definition comes straight from an on-line dictionary:

- a regimen of eating and drinking sparingly so as to reduce one's weight

My favourite definition also comes from the same dictionary:

- food and drink regularly provided or consumed
- habitual nourishment

Look at the last two definitions and you will see the words 'regularly provided and consumed' and 'habitual'. So don't think of diet as a short-term fix. The 'ideal diet' is a pattern of consumption that is sustainable. So forget the hundreds of super weight loss diet programs. Skip those channels on TV and just get yourself into a regimen of healthy eating. Some things you may consider:

- Manage your total calorie input. The average man needs around 2300 calories per day and the average woman 2000 calories. If you are not exercising and consuming more than this then your weight is likely to go up. Keep your calories at a level close to these numbers. If you increase your activity levels substantially then you may, over time, need to change your diet, but let it be 'on demand' rather than 'in advance'.

- Balance your diet. I love the concept that a friend of mine from India showed me. Draw a circle and imagine it is your meal plate. First draw a line down the centre; the right half of the circle represents the proportion of vegetables in your diet. Split the remaining half so you have 2 quarters. In one quarter you have protein or meat and the final quarter carbohydrates, potato or rice for example. As long as your plate is a reasonable size and you keep the fat levels low then this is a simple way to keep balance.

- Eat breakfast. Skipping breakfast is one of the worst things you can do in dietary terms. Eating breakfast does a number of things that are really beneficial to you:
  o It kick-starts your metabolism and gets your digestive system active. Your body's burn rate will increase.
  o It provides the necessary energy for the first part of your day.

- Eat more fresh food. Cut down on tinned and processed food as additives and preservatives may take away some of the goodness and natural taste. Head to the fresh food sections in the supermarket and spend a little more time preparing your own food. That way you know exactly what you're eating!

- Eat less fat, especially saturated and animal fats.

- Watch the number of take outs and deliveries. Pizza, fried chicken and burgers are the heart of many evils, especially if you are inactive and have a tendency to put on weight. If you are hooked, then seriously reduce the number of these meals you have in any given week.

This may look challenging and it will require some significant changes in some of your habits, but the benefits are huge: you'll have more energy, look great, feel great and have the opportunity to live longer! Just remember that nothing worth having ever comes easy.

Plan 13 – Looking after myself

Specific actions I will take to improve my overall health:

Activity actions

    1. ____

    2. ____

    3. ____

Nutrition actions

    1. ____

    2. ____

    3. ____

Benefits

    1. ____________________________

    2. ____________________________

    3. ____________________________

14. Look after your money

"If you don't look after your money then someone else will!"
Anon

As the old saying goes "A fool and their money are easily parted". Money doesn't necessarily make the world go round, but as a friend of mine once said to me "I've been broke and rich, if you haven't tried being rich then give it a go, it's fun!" The starting point of any plan to increase your relative wealth is to look after your money; the second is to increase your income by improving yourself, starting a business and so on. We'll start the process off by looking at how you can best manage what you have.

I have discovered by reading, practising, and making a few big mistakes, some really effective rules on looking after your money. If you want to get into more depth, then buy a book on the subject. Here is my simple list of 'always' and 'never' guidelines;

Always:
- put aside at least 10% of your pay check every month into a long term investment – in addition to your pension
- keep six months of disposable income in a quick access account for a rainy day – lost job, illness, emergency
- have a pension plan – plan and invest from the day you start your first job
- save up for vacations, and non-essentials – if you dreamed of owning a Harley-Davidson motorcycle then open a 'Harley account' and put a few dollars in it every month
- use a debit card not a credit card – it will encourage you to only spend what you have
- grow your net worth as a measure of your success rather than your income – you can earn more and spend more and be no better off. It is more effective to measure how much your net worth increases i.e. your assets minus your liabilities. For example: an asset would be a property or investments and liabilities your mortgage and other debt

- pay off high interest loans/borrowing first – clear credit cards before mortgages or other lower cost borrowing
- clear credit card balance at the end of each month, even if you have to dip into short-term savings to do so – it is probably the most expensive borrowing you will ever have

Never:
- build up debt on a depreciating asset - don't borrow money to buy a car, save for one instead. A new car will depreciate the minute you drive it out of the dealership and the credit costs will be high. Better to drive an old car and save for a new one. In fact buying a one year old car makes the best sense as it's gone through its biggest depreciation already!
- use a credit card for day-to-day expenses, use a debit card instead. If you don't have the money in your account then don't spend!
- borrow money for a vacation – when the vacation is over the payments will continue!
- borrow money from a friend – one day it may cost you your friendship.
- invest in get-rich-quick schemes - there is always a catch and very, very rarely a real payback. The only person who is likely to get rich quick, is the person running the scheme!
- waste small amounts of money. They build up to big amounts over time. For example, if you buy a coffee every working day from a typical big coffee outlet, the cost per day might be just $4. That's $1,040 per annum. Invested at 6% pa, that would be worth over $160,000 over your working lifetime! "Fancy a cappuccino?" "No thanks, I'll make one myself!"

So now you are doing a great job of looking after your existing money, how about thinking bigger in terms of your move to those bigger goals of financial independence or even wealth? The simplest way I can find to do this is to give you the attributes of financially independent and wealthy people and let you compare yourselves to them. This is fairly unscientific, but I have studied well and I think you will see the common themes:

- They are action oriented – they see opportunity and grab it
- They have clear goals – usually in written lists
- They spend less than they earn
- They pay cash for all except appreciating assets
- They invest as much as they can reasonably manage
- They are self-confident and self-motivated
- They tend to be business owners and/or investors
- They take calculated risks
- They pay themselves first – the first items to come out of a pay check are their investments
- They take advice – from accountants and professionals
- They cut out the middle man – they have direct relationships with suppliers and partners
- They focus on what they need rather than what they want
- They are often creative and ask questions to challenge conventional thinking
- If they are business owners then their businesses are usually simple – buy low and sell high
- They take great care with their money and are often seen as thrifty

I also believe that being wealthy or being poor starts with your attitude and how you see yourself. As Mike Todd once famously said "I've never been poor, only broke. Being poor is a state of mind but being broke is only a temporary situation!"

Plan 14 – Looking after my money

Specific actions I will take to look after my money:

1. ____

____

____

2. ____

____

____

3. ____

____

____

4. ____

____

____

5. ____

____

____

My personal financial 'always' and 'never' list

I will always	I will never

15. Don't try

"Do or do not. There is no try!"
Yoda to Luke Skywalker, when he dared to suggest to the Jedi coach
that he would 'try' to levitate his X wing fighter (from Star Wars)

Clear message from Yoda then: if it's worth doing, then do it, and if it isn't then don't do it, but don't ever pick the middle road of trying. How do you feel when you ask someone a question and you get the 'T' word back? Look at these;

- Steve: "Hey, can you make it to our party on Saturday"
  Suzy: "Not sure yet, but I'll try"

- Helen: "Don't forget I need that report tonight"
  David: "I haven't forgotten, I'll do what I can"

- Jeanie: "Dad, can you get home early tonight so we can go to the movies"
  Dad: "I'm real busy at work, but I'll try"

- Anne: "I hear you're going to run a Marathon!"
  Eddie: "Yeah, I'm sure going to give it a try!"

I'll bet you that Suzy, David, Dad and Eddie didn't succeed in their commitments and guess why? The answer is in their half-hearted responses. Even if the 'T' word isn't present as in the second example, the language is not that of a commitment to the result.

The most appalling thing you can do in the pursuit of your goals is to 'try'. The language gives you an opportunity to back out and you are going to use it as, and most likely, when, you feel it is appropriate. We have become almost immune to the word and many use it on a daily basis and get the results that go along with it.

Successful people, whether it is in sport, business, home life or not-for-profit work, rarely use anything other than positive language. When did you last hear the world's greatest golfer, sprinter, motor racer, skier, or high jumper, state in the media that they were going to 'try' in the next competition? The people you may hear that from will be the sports people lower down the ranks who talk about how good their competition is, how challenging it is going to be to beat them, but how they are going to try and give it their best shot. Guess where they will still be in 2-3 years' time?

When Usain Bolt decided to break all of those world sprint records at 100m and 200m, he did not try, he just plain did it! When Michael Schumacher decided to become a motor racing legend, there was no doubt in his mind and he never ever 'tried'! When Sir Richard Branson decided to become a world leader in entrepreneurship and business, he did not think about trying!

So what makes you use that word? Check out the list below and see where you may have caught the 'try bug':

- Fear of saying 'no'. You may find it easier to say 'maybe' or 'try' when asked to do something than to come straight out and say 'no'. If this is you then think of nicer ways to say 'no'. "I'd love to come to the party, but I promised to spend some time with my family this weekend"

- Not motivated to take the action. Maybe the goal is not yours and you're just going through the motions? Review your goals and decide on each. Choose whether you want to pursue the goal or not. If you are not sure, scrap it!

- Lack of confidence in your own ability to achieve the objective. This is the real rub of why the 'T' word seems to be so prevalent these days. Just like in Star Wars when Yoda said those fateful words to Luke Skywalker, it is not others that can really hold you back, it is you. Personal commitment will get you bigger and greater achievements in all areas of your life if you simply have the belief that you can do it!

- You tried once and failed. So you had a bad experience and this is causing self-doubt. It is time to rebuild your confidence and remember that failure is only final when you give up! Remove your self-doubt and achieve your goals. It really is that easy.

The worst enemy of achievement is a lack of commitment. Be committed and just do it!

Plan 15 – My language

Specific actions I will take to avoid the 'bad' words, like 'try' and 'attempt':

1. _______________________________________
   ____
   ____
2. _______________________________________
   ____
   ____
3. _______________________________________
   ____
   ____

Specific actions I will take to remove self-doubt:

1. _______________________________________
   ____
   ____
2. _______________________________________
   ____
   ____
3. _______________________________________
   ____
   ____

Hint:
- Remind myself of past achievements
- Celebrate every small success
- Talk to myself
- Be with positive people

16. Yes, I Can!

"Whether you think you can, whether you think you can't, you are right!"
Henry Ford

Maybe, not sure, not easy, too hard, too old, not fit enough, not clever enough, DNA isn't right, not possible, can't…. If your responses to challenges in life sit inside this collection then guess what? Yes, you got it, you cannot and will not achieve your full potential. As Henry Ford succinctly put it: - "you become the result of your self-fulfilling prophecy. If you think you can, then you will, if you think you can't then you won't."

When people get the 'yes, I can' bug, they become unstoppable and get to be the ones who prove to the world that the seemingly difficult or impossible things can be done!

- Despite numerous 'failures', Roger Bannister had this stubborn belief that it was possible to run a mile in under 4 minutes and that he was the person to do it. This was after coming a poor 4th in the 1952 Olympics and almost quitting running altogether. Eventually Bannister made the mental decision that he was going to be the person to break the 9 year old world record of 4 minutes 1.4 seconds. Many of the rest of the running community, joined by sportswriters and commentators, declared it 'impossible'. This egged Bannister on even more. On the 6th May 1954 Bannister set a time of 3:59.4 and demonstrated that it was indeed possible. Since that landmark day and Bannister's proof that it was possible to run under 4 minutes the record dropped progressively and now stands at 3:43.13, over 16 seconds less than the first sub 4 minute record. I wonder if anyone is looking at 3:40 or even 3:30!

- Until he was 22, Paul J Meyer, the son of German immigrant parents, failed at pretty much everything he did. He made numerous mistakes in his early life, but rarely repeated any. His incredible 'yes, I can' attitude took him through all of his life's challenges. As a young insurance agent he saw every door that was closed in his face as an opportunity to keep the next door open in his bid to become the best insurance salesman on the planet. His first step towards that was at the tender age of 22 when he became the youngest ever member of the Million Dollar Round Table (MDRT) - the insurance industries global success recognition body. By the age of 27 he had made over $1,000,000 in the insurance business, and that was in 1955. Five years later he started Success Motivation Inc. and went on to develop numerous personal development programs that have become staple reading for thousands. Late into his thirties he decided to learn to play tennis and became one of the best players in Texas in his forties. Pretty much everything he went into was a success, mostly based on an absolute determination and an underlying 'yes, I can' attitude!

- One of the greatest 'yes, I can' people I know proves this attitude in a spectacular manner. Rajesh Durbal was born with bones missing in both legs and his right arm. In his first year of life both of his legs were amputated, so he became a triple amputee with just one full limb, his left arm. During his early life he struggled with his disability but in 2009 he made an incredible decision. He chose to demonstrate to himself and the world what was possible with an energy, determination and level of self-belief like no other! He spent hours and hours building and modifying prosthetic limbs to prepare to run a 5km race. This was merely a stepping stone because just one year after setting his goal – (a year of training days and nights, of building and maintaining his prosthetics), he competed in and finished the Hawaii Ironman race. Never heard of Ironman? It is a 2.4 mile ocean swim followed by a 112 mile cycle ride, followed by a full 26.2 mile run. Rajesh completed this in 14 hours 19 minutes and 13 seconds. Now that is what I call a 'yes I can' attitude!

So repeat after me:

"Can I run a successful business? Yes, I can"

"Can I write a bestselling book? Yes, I can"

"Can I be a great parent? Yes, I can"

"Can I run a marathon? Yes, I can"

"Can I get an MBA? Yes, I can"

Can't never achieved anything!

Plan 16 – Yes I can!

Write down a few of your current 'can't' issues then use positive language to demonstrate why you CAN.

Can't	Yes I can

Example:

Can't – I can't write well enough to be an author

Can – I can write a bestselling novel and I will start creative writing lessons in 3 weeks!

17. It's never too late

Now these are some of the wisest words that ring true to me. When you hear words like "I'm too old for that", "it's too late", "not in my lifetime"-what you're really hearing are excuses. Age is an arbitrary number. It is simply the number of laps we have done around that large fiery object we call our Sun. The first 18 laps we are at school the next few laps we may go to college, then the middle 40 laps we work. Then we retire for as many laps as we can manage until we die. Sounds awful doesn't it? Well it's never too late to start dreaming and setting new goals!

As I write this book I am 64, and on my 5th career. I'm an ultra-distance runner, cyclist, Ironman tri-athlete, kayaker and multi-sport athlete. I race hard and beat many who are 20 years younger than I am. I'm a musician, leadership coach, facilitator, motivational speaker and an author. I'm also a photographer, glider pilot, boat captain and entrepreneur. I published my first book in 2008. I own two businesses and have made it onto the Amazon International bestseller list twice in the last three years! I also plan to sail around the world in the next 10 years. However, I'm an amateur by comparison to these people!

- At the age of 65 Colonel Sanders struggled when a bypass forced him to close his only restaurant and gas station in Corbin, Kentucky. He was not downhearted though and went on the road with his only asset: his secret ingredient fried chicken recipe. By his 70th birthday he had established over 190 franchisees with 400 operating units in the USA and Canada.

- Although Sam Walton ran a number of successful retail stores in his early years, it wasn't until 1962 at the age of 44 that he started Wal-Mart and got firmly on the road to building the world's largest retailer. In the intervening years he experimented with different markets, locations and business models. By the time Wal-Mart was formed he knew what worked and what didn't. He had also learned the hard way, with a number of 'failures' in his attempts to learn and remodel the retail business. This early learning is almost certainly what caused the rapid rise of the Wal-Mart chain with few, if any, notable problems. Sam's net worth when he died aged 74 in 1992 was just under US$60 billion - a fortune he had built in just 30 years from US$20,000.

On the subject of physical fitness take a look at these great old-timers:

- The world's oldest mountain guide, Ulrich Inderbinen, who died at age 103, was a resident of Zermatt, in Switzerland. He built his own home in the 1930s and for seven decades did without the use of a car or telephone or bicycle, serving on Swiss ski patrols during World War II, and labouring as a carpenter, electrician and lumberjack. As European holidays and alpine adventures gained in popularity, Inderbinen supported his family through mountain guide work. This became his full-time job and passion. He made his last, of more than 370 Matterhorn climbs, shortly before his 90th birthday. He gave up ski guiding at 95, and mountain guiding at 97. He quit, when he realized he had taken 10 minutes longer than he should have, to descend the Breithorn, a 13,600-foot peak near Zermatt. He lived for another six years after he retired.

- One of the world's more mature marathon runners, Granny Luces, ran her first marathon at the age of 56 in her home country of Trinidad in the West Indies. She is a mother of 11, has numerous grandchildren and even a couple of great grandchildren. In 2008 she ran a marathon in 6 hours 21 minutes at the ripe old age of 81. In a 2005 interview when she was a youthful 78, she was quoted as saying: "I have about 17 golds [from international races]. I run all over the world you know: Rome, Australia, Oregon, San Francisco, Puerto Rico. Anytime they have race anywhere in Trinidad, I am ready." She also has a race named after her called 'The Granny Luces 15km'. Her indomitable attitude gets others hooked on the sport and she is famous for finishing every race she has ever started, while leaving many youngsters in her wake. "It is very good to be running. It takes away stress, you know. After I train and come home, I just feel like I'm the only person in the world and everything is good and nothing is bad. I always tell people about that."

- Werner Berger is in the Guinness book of world records for being the oldest man to complete the ascent of the seven highest mountains on the seven continents. He topped Everest as a sprightly 69 year old in 2007. He's also planning to do the same again before he is 90. Last I heard he was on top of Kilimanjaro in Africa celebrating his 80th Birthday!

It also appears that creativity can show up much later in life. Take a look at some of these success stories:

- Mary Wesley, author of the *Camomile Lawn*, didn't publish her first adult novel until she was 70 but then went on to become one of Britain's most successful novelists, publishing her last book in 2001 a year before her death at age 90.

- Annie Proulx (author of *the Shipping News* and *Brokeback Mountain*) didn't start writing until in her 50s. At age 58 she won the PEN/Faulkner book award, for her debut novel. The following year she won a Pulitzer Prize for *The Shipping News*. *Brokeback Mountain* became a huge worldwide success when the film was released in 2007.

- Celebrated Irish painter, Tony O'Malley, taught himself to paint while working for more than 25 years as a bank official. He was almost 40 before he started exhibiting his work and he went on painting for the rest of his life. He died aged 90 in 2003.

- American Artist, Bill Traylor, did not begin to draw until he was 83. In the following few years, he produced over 1800 drawings and was discovered after he started hanging his works of art on a fence to amuse his friends. He carried on drawing until his death aged 95.
- Back closer to home, my grandfather got his first degree at age 80 and wrote his first book two years later!

It truly is never too late to start pursuing your goals!

Plan 17 – My future

A list of my possible future careers:

Career	Action	By when

Hint:
Write three lists
1. *The things you love to do – your passions*
2. *The things you are good at – your power*
3. *The things that are important to you – your priorities*

When you look at these you will find links that may guide you on your future career(s).

An example
1. *Passion - I love working with people*
2. *Power - I have been good at it in the past and can develop myself further to be great at it*
3. *Priority - It will give me flexibility in my schedule and enable me to do something I love. I can also earn a decent living doing it.*

18. Don't ever, ever give up

"Run when you can, walk when you have to and crawl when you must, but never, ever, give up!"
Dean Karnazes

Dean coined this phrase to help him through some of his huge physical and mental challenges, when training for and participating in his 50/50/50 challenge. The objective was to run 50 26.2 mile marathons in 50 US states in 50 consecutive days. Yes, you heard it right, that's 1,310 miles of running. Of course, he completed the challenge running the 50th, the New York Marathon, in a few seconds over 3 hours. He has many other running records to his credit including running 350 miles in just under 89 hours. He has now run many more miles, several deserts and a few mountains. If you really want to tire yourself out then take a look at his typical racing and training schedule and then consider actually doing it!

When you look at people like Karnazes and other major achievers in the world of endurance sports, it's tough to spot the difference between them and an 'ordinary' individual. They may look a little fitter, but then there are people who look similar and compete, but just don't make it to the end.

The difference between success at their sport and another's relative failure may not be visible, but it does exist. The reason that you can't see it is because it's all in the mind! It is that downright stubbornness and inability to accept failure that drives people like him on to extraordinary achievement. Sure it requires miles and miles of training, commitment to give up every day regular things and an unerring desire to achieve the end result. But, on the day of the event, there is only one objective: to FINISH!

My longest race distance at the time of publishing this book is 56 miles. At the time of doing my first I had never run more than 35 miles in training, so there were 21 miles of unknown territory. On race day in June 2007 in South Africa I felt great. I had trained to the schedule, was injury free and just looking forward to the race. I had my pace charts that showed me my times for each key stage of the race and I planned to execute to perfection, as I had the confidence in the advice I had been given by my fellow racers who were 'old timers' at this distance. The start gun went and I set off at my prescribed pace and started clocking off the distance markers which measured a countdown to the finish. As I approached the marker that signified 21 miles to the finish, I realised I was in unknown territory, I had never in my life run this distance before.

I felt great in myself, but within minutes I felt a twinge in my left calf, my right hip joint felt sore, and in no time at all, I was a running wreck and my mind began playing tricks. "Well you've proved a point, you can stop now and nobody will question you"; "you've run further than anyone you know, you've done it"; "look, there are some other people who have stopped, you can stop too!"

I realised then that there was only one thing that could stop me in this race and that was my mind. The minor pains had been there all along, they just got bigger because my mind told me that they were bigger. It was all a conspiracy! Now that I was aware of what was happening the rest was easy. I started to push out the aches and pains and see the finish line with the cheering crowds. I was shouting at myself - yes, out loud - , "this is a running race damn it, you can't walk", "I came here to run and finish!" And so it came true: 20 minutes ahead of schedule with 9 hours and 40 minutes of running and I crossed the finish line with the biggest piece of learning in my life: in most things, the only person who can stop you succeeding is yourself! I nearly talked myself out of one of the most rewarding experiences in my life.

Dean's running statement can, of course, be applied to all areas of your life. If you have decided on your goal and are determined to achieve it, the only thing that is likely to stop you is yourself. So think and metaphorically run towards your goal. If you can no longer run, then walk, and if you cannot walk then crawl and do whatever you can to keep moving in that direction, but never, ever, ever, give up!

Here are some of my personal favourites in the 'never, ever give up' arena:

- Walt Disney's first attempts at drawing cartoons were ridiculed by the press and his first business went bankrupt. The Disney empire is now a $30 billion business.

- UK wartime Prime Minister Winston Churchill failed his 6th grade, but persevered, finished school and went on to be one of the most highly regarded leaders of the 20th Century.

- A school teacher who had a dream to hit the big time as an author went through rejection after rejection and actually got to the point of dumping a manuscript in the garbage. Fortunately his resolute wife fished it out, he completed it and they sent it to another publisher. An advance came back for $2,500 and eventually the book earned over $400,000. The book was Carrie and the author was Stephen King!

- You have to love the quote from Michael Jordan, the world famous basketball player who went home and cried when he was cut from his high school team: "I've missed more than 9000 shots in my career. I've lost almost 300 games. Twenty-six times I've been trusted to take the game winning shot and missed. I've failed over and over and over again in my life. And that is why I succeed!"

- Finally, and probably the most famous of all, Thomas Edison's dogged determination to find a material that would form the filament for the electric light bulb. Scientific records suggest that he tried over 3000 different variations of materials before he got it right. Every time he tried a new material and it failed he saw it merely as feedback, not failure.

Those who do give up have been relegated to 'also ran' more often than not, because they simply don't realise that every failure is to be celebrated, as it takes you nearer to success! Honestly, if you've never failed, you've never lived!

Plan 18 - Affirmations

Dean's run, walk, and crawl chant is a form of affirmation. Develop a couple for yourself and use when you need to talk yourself into taking action on your goals. For example if your goal relates to eating a more healthy diet and exercising regularly then your affirmation may be something like "I love my body and I'm going to make it last!" or "I am fit and healthy!"

Some words and affirmations I can use that support my own goals:

Goal	Affirmation

19. Live a wide life

"I don't want to get to the end of my life and find that I lived just the length of it. I want to have lived the width of it as well."
Diane Ackerman

Now there is a statement I can live with and embrace. Wouldn't it be a shame to get to the end of your days and to still have that yearning that you wished you had done something that you never got around to? Well, the dream and goal setting guidance should get you thinking in the right direction, and planning and prioritising should help you achieve what you have set out to do, but given that we only typically use a small piece of our potential, you might ask whether you are really stretching yourself to see, feel and experience new things. Think about Goddard's life list of 127 goals and ask yourself whether you are really living life to the fullest and making the most of that sleeping giant that is your untapped potential.

Go back and look at your dream list. Put crazy things on it that just simply appeals to your childlike side. Be frivolous - even for a moment. Remember, just writing down your goals is not yet a commitment to achieving them. Even John Goddard dismissed some of his goals after he had reviewed them. One of his early goals, "Appear in a Tarzan movie" never made it into his action items, but no doubt if it had, he would have made it come true!

How you measure width may produce some interesting challenges, but you could certainly ask yourself some of these questions:

- How can I really use more of my potential – mental, physical, emotional, or spiritual?

- If I had a clean sheet of paper, what would I write on it that depicts an ideal life?

- I may have lots of 'things', but which of these would I happily give up to get new 'experiences'?

For example, at some point, you may decide to sell your house and sail around the world or forget the inheritance for your kids and plough your time and efforts into charitable work. After all, on the subject of money and possessions, you can't take it with you when you go.

Of course, how wide you decide to make your life is personal and as we have already outlined, that choice lies only with you! John Goddard's view is about as wide as it gets, just look at some of his 'wide' activities:

- He explored the Nile, Amazon, Congo, Colorado and Rio Coco rivers.

- He studied life and lived amongst tribes in 11 regions including New Guinea, Borneo and The Sudan.

- He climbed 12 of the world's highest and most dramatic peaks including the Matterhorn, Mt Fuji and Kilimanjaro.

- He visited over 120 countries in the world.

- He was a deep sea diver, master pilot, explorer, skier (water and snow); published books; ran sub 5 minute miles; was fluent in English, Spanish and Arabic; read all of Shakespeare's combined works and most of the Encyclopaedia Britannica and the list goes on.

John isn't unique either, there are lists of great achievers all around you from different backgrounds who have pursued diverse passions. Some of them started young like John and many other discovered adventure at a much later time in their lives.

 Live Life Now – Rethink 1440

On the inside front and back covers you can see some of the things that I have achieved as well as some future goals. My view of 'wide' may not be as global as John's but more based around what I can achieve mentally, emotionally, spiritually and physically. My list of 'things to do' gets even longer and more challenging on a daily basis, but these words continue to rattle through my head almost daily: The point of life isn't to arrive at your final destination well preserved and in pristine condition, but rather to slide in sideways, tired, burnt out and totally spent, yelling, "Holy cow, what a ride!"

Plan 19 – My 'wide' life goals

Think about some 'wide' life experiences and consider how important it is to you given you are now a decisive person who makes better choices! Maybe you want to swim with dolphins, climb the Matterhorn or sip champagne watching the Aurora Borealis. Now's the time to start the list!

Some of my 'wide' life desires that I must experience:

Experience	When

20. Be grateful!

And don't forget to smell the roses on your journey through the garden. Achievement isn't just about goals and the blind pursuit of things. It is more about how it makes you feel and experiencing your positive effect on others. Goals are important. Without them, we can end up wandering aimlessly through life. What matters most is the feeling we get as a result of achieving them as well as the journey towards that success. One of the highest levels of human need is that of self-actualisation or fulfilment.

What we have to be grateful for also depends on our life situation. I always had this burning desire to fly and eventually I learnt to fly a glider and I remember that incredible feeling of silence and freedom that it gave. Sometime after I was reminded of a different view of life when a friend of mine in South Africa with Cerebral Palsy talked to me about how he dreamed of walking, something most of us take for granted daily.

Picture this:

- A cancer survivor who dreams that the next scan is 'all clear'
- A wheelchair bound boy who dreams of playing football
- A woman who dreams of a relationship where she is not abused
- A blind man who dreams of seeing a sunset
- An unemployed labourer who dreams of a job

And so the list goes on.

Gratitude is not really as simple as wandering around saying 'thanks' to people. It is far deeper than that and definitely not a mechanical process. It's more of an attitude or feeling that people simply sense when they are around you. Sure you are very unlikely to be a complainer; so generally, it is what's within you that makes the difference. True 'attitude of gratitude' people are pretty easy to spot:

- They rarely complain.
- They see the good in everybody.
- The word 'hate' does not exist in their vocabulary.
- They make lots of choices and accept the outcome.
- They accept personal responsibility and don't blame external circumstances or people.
- There is a content, 'at peace' air about them.
- They are givers and will often help other people ahead of helping themselves.
- They don't bear grudges.
- They are flexible and embrace change.
- They are confident, yet humble.
- They are sincere when they say 'please' and 'thank you'!

These are some of my 'attitude of gratitude' heroes:

- Oseola McCarty lived her life in Hattiesburg, Mississippi and after her Aunt became bedridden and she had to give up school she spent most of her life washing people's clothes. On the surface a quite unremarkable existence, but this is where the story gets amazing. Left to fend for herself from a young age she lived a simple and frugal life: she spent only what she needed and saved the rest. A few dollars here and there went into her savings accounts. At the age of 86 she had to stop work due to arthritis. It was at this stage that she decided to figure out what to do with her life savings that had amounted to a staggering $250,000. Clearly she could have lived a life of luxury as she faced retirement, however, she chose a different use for her life savings. The first challenge for the bank trustees was to help her understand the enormity of her fortune as she had only ever managed a few dollars. The trustee used coins to represent her savings, a dime being 10% and so on. In the end she chose one dime (10%) for her church, one dime (10%) for each of her 3 relatives and the remaining 6 dimes (60%) for the University of Southern Mississippi (USM). This final bequest of $150,000 was to be used to fund the tertiary education of African-American youths who could not afford to pay tuition due to financial hardship. In 1996 Harvard recognised her with an honorary doctorate and President Bill Clinton awarded her the Presidential Citizens Medal. Many youngsters benefitted from her kindness before she died in 1999, aged 91 years. Many more have benefitted from her legacy since then and she will forever be remembered for her simple generosity.

- Motivational speaker and author, Keith Harrell, who sadly passed away in 2010, was famous for his positive and thankful attitude. I remember seeing him being interviewed and being asked about how he remained so positive. "Easy", he said, "if I ever feel a little low in the morning I look at the obituary column in the local paper. It reminds me that I woke up above ground today and they didn't". Right up to his passing he remained one of the most positive people on the planet. I'm sure he understood the irony of his famous quote on that final day!

- Dick Traum lost his right leg when he was just 24 in a car accident in a gas station. Rather than feeling sorry for himself he chose to be grateful for what he had and in 1976 he went on to become the first amputee to complete the New York Marathon with a prosthetic. Having realised the positive effect that this had on him he then went on to found the Achilles Track Club. Through the club, and its over 150 chapters in 60 countries, he encourages, and coaches people with disabilities to train for, and complete, races of all types. The purpose of Achilles has always been to integrate athletes with disabilities into mainstream events. "When an able-bodied runner gets passed by someone who is blind or on one leg, it changes their perception of what the disabled can do," Traum says. He is the ultimate motivator and a master goal-setting coach. His simple request of his athletes: "Put the date in your diary; it is the day when you will be running the New York Marathon. Now let's get training".

The complainers will always be around, they just don't understand the effect they have on others. Remember that in any situation that makes you unhappy you always have three choices:

1. Learn to live with it
2. Work to positively change it
3. Leave

As you read before that there is no fourth choice to moan, whine and complain!

Plan 20 – Be grateful

Attitude of Gratitude Actions

10 things I am grateful for in my life: e.g. I am healthy, I have great family....

1. _______________________________
2. _______________________________
3. _______________________________
4. _______________________________
5. _______________________________
6. _______________________________
7. _______________________________
8. _______________________________
9. _______________________________
10. ______________________________

Five things I am going to do to change my attitude e.g. Stop complaining.

1. _______________________________
2. _______________________________
3. _______________________________
4. _______________________________
5. _______________________________

Write down 3 things to be grateful for every night!

1. _______________________________
2. _______________________________
3. _______________________________

21 Attitude is everything!

"Attitude is a little thing that makes a big difference!"
Winston Churchill

Of course the big difference that it makes depends on whether your attitude is positive or negative. I recently did a search on Amazon.com on the words 'Attitude is Everything' and found almost 400 entries. Surely, if 400 books have been written on and around that subject then it must be true. If attitude is everything and I have a great positive attitude, does that guarantee my success? Let's take a few minutes to test the statement and see if it really stands up to its claim.

What is attitude? The dictionary gives us the following definition:

Noun: attitude - A complex mental state involving beliefs and feelings and values and dispositions to act in certain ways e.g. "he had the attitude that work was fun!"

Attitude is most commonly known as the state of mind that creates behavior. Simply put, our actions are driven by our thoughts and our thoughts are what determine our attitude. As our attitude drives our behavior, then a negative attitude creates negative behaviors and a positive attitude creates positive behaviors.

That does not mean that a negative attitude makes a bad person, just that their view of life is intensely different to that of a positive person. The old adage of how people see a glass as 'half empty versus half full' is a good example of that. In fact, to a really positive person their glass isn't just half full it is overflowing with opportunity! Typically, a person with a positive attitude has an internal drive and recognizes their own role in their success. A person with a negative attitude is much more likely to blame external circumstances for their failure to achieve and not hold themselves accountable for their success.

Our current attitude is actually the result of a complex mixture of pretty much everything that has happened to us in the past. A positive attitude is likely to have come about as a result of a set of positive experiences, a positive role model or parent, or even in our peer group or school. Various studies show that over 90% of our behaviour and attitude today is a result of our past conditioning and less than 10% is what we are born with. So our attitude is something we have learnt rather than something we have been born with. The good news is that, if you have a poor or negative attitude, then you can change and learn new positive attitudes and, as such, behaviours! Psychologist and philosopher William James summed it up like this: "The greatest discovery of my generation is that human beings can alter their lives by altering their attitudes of mind."

So, attitude is something, but is it everything?

I have met and am pleased to know many people with very positive attitudes. I like to think of it as the 'Yes, I can!' view of life. They always see the best side of everyone and every situation, good or bad, as an opportunity. When it rains, they think about how the garden needed it; if they lose their job, they see it as an opportunity to do something different. When you meet them and ask how they are, you always get "great", "good" or even "super fantastic". They always seem to be genuinely happy about their situation and life, even if it is not filled with the riches that some see as a measure of success.

When I meet successful people, I always examine their attitude, which is invariably positive. I have yet to meet a truly successful person with a bad or negative attitude. I have, however, seen negative attitudes cripple otherwise talented individuals. At some point in their climb to success, in any area of life, their negative attitude creeps in and self-doubt or fear of failure clips their wings and the slippery slope to mediocrity begins.

If you feel your attitude could do with a helping hand, then here are some simple guidelines that can help you:

- Mix with positive people and avoid the doom merchants
- Read motivational and positive books and articles
- Celebrate small victories that you achieve on the way towards your goals
- Exercise more – yes, it's true, exercise improves your attitude!

- Remind yourself of your achievements and keep mementoes of them
- Talk to yourself! Remind yourself of your 'can do' attitude using positive affirmations
- Spend your time doing as many things that you love to do and follow the things that you are passionate about
- Change your language. Swap out words like 'try', 'should' and 'hope' with 'do', 'will' and 'can'

One of the biggest ways to measure your attitude is to reflect on what happens when you encounter challenges, especially due to circumstances outside of your control. Let me share a story of an experience I had while preparing to swim long races.

In 2014 I decided to do a big swim race. It was 3.5 miles around Gasparee, one of the southernmost islands off Trinidad, in the Caribbean, which I now call home. I had never swum that distance before and the conditions were tough but I felt confident. With nervousness not completely eliminated I started and off we headed east, across the north of the island. Open water swimming requires 'sighting'. Maybe once every 10-15 swim strokes you pop your head up to make sure you are on the right course. Swimming off course is a big danger and you can expend huge amounts of energy getting back on course as well as moving out of the protection of the kayakers who are supporting you.

The swim progressed well as I headed over to the North East of the island in good conditions. I saw other swimmers around me so was confident and felt strong and in the groove. There were a few light waves that were a little uncomfortable as they were coming from my left, and as a 'lefty' breather, since I breathe every other stroke on my left side, I was getting the odd mouth full of water. No stress though...it was all good.

I noticed the island to my right moving away which meant I had to gradually swim a little closer to the island as we started to turn South near an old Fort. I was told in my training, that at this point I would feel some head-on current and maybe even headwinds and waves. Sure enough as I started to head South I felt bigger waves head-on and also noticed something strange: as I sighted the island on my right I noticed a big rock just past the Fort which didn't seem to be moving. Head back down another couple of minutes, and I look up and see the same rock in the same place. A sudden realization flooded over me: the wind, waves and current were all head-on and I was not moving forward despite my strong efforts.

I decided to pull faster strokes and kick harder. I gave it maybe 5-10 minutes and then looked up. To my horror I was still seeing the same rock I had sighted much earlier. On top of which, all this energy exertion was starting to tire me out, and for a short while I was pushed backwards.

I remember in my earlier chats with the experienced swimmers, many said they had to be pulled from the water for the same reasons I was now experiencing first hand. I looked around and saw some swimmers a little further away from the island, maybe 50 yards away. They were making slow but steady progress and that was inspiring. I realized that getting closer to the island meant experiencing a stronger current. I could overcome the current or the wind and waves but not both. It went against all my instincts to swim off the shortest line but right now I couldn't get past that damn rock and if I kept doing the same thing then I would be pulled from the water by the safety boats following another 20-30 minutes of exhaustion.

This is what I decided to do: I slowly adjusted my path, to move further left and away from the island. As I looked up I saw that I was actually going backwards at one point and the rock was 50-60 yards ahead. The lost ground was messing with me and I was overwhelmed with self-doubt. I looked at the nearby Kayak and thought about raising an arm; the universal sign for 'I'm done, come and get me'. I started talking to myself and using my well-worn affirmation 'I am a swimming monster' to push myself on. I winced at the cramp in my right calf and pulled my foot in to prevent it knotting. I got my head back down and ground away and after what seemed like an eternity, I saw the rock again. This time it was moving... backwards. I was finally passing the rock!

The old adage of the definition of insanity: doing the same thing over and over and expecting a different result, holds true. Of course, you have figured out already the message behind this story. To make progress in all areas of life, and I mean real progress, means a constant state of change: change in goals, change in behaviour, change in attitude, change in what you do and how you do it, with a constant reminder to yourself of why you are doing what you are doing. In other words, what is your driving motivation.

Planning is definitely a key to success when setting goals, but you can't always plan for every obstacle. I have to say that I am not a fan of the concept of having a plan 'b' just in case plan 'a' doesn't work. My experience is that it can take away your focus from the original plan and working flat out on the achievement of that goal using the planned methodology. I do believe that prior to taking on a goal it is worth doing a 'what is the best that can happen' exercise and then taking a look at how to improve the chances of it happening. Then doing a 'what is the worst that can happen' and mitigating the risk.

Your own personal 'rock' and your goal will determine your approach to dealing with potential issues. There is one element that can't be planned for and that really is your determination and persistence to complete the goal. There are two elements to that, firstly your personal 'why':- what is your burning desire to achieve the goal. The second is

 Live Life Now – Rethink 1440

just that plain hard headed stubbornness - an attitude that refuses to let you stop.

So, is attitude really everything? Well in the context of achieving results in all areas of your life it has to be at the very top of your success criteria. The evidence is totally overwhelming regardless of where you sit. Without a doubt - great effort, great results and great success spring from having a great attitude!

Plan 21 – Building a positive attitude

Specific actions I will take to build my positive attitude:

1. ____

   ____

2. ____

   ____

3. ____

   ____

4. ____

   ____

5. ____

   ____

   ____

Hint:
Refer to previous chapters and look at things like:
- List your achievements
- Read 'attitude' books
- Hang around with positive people
- Celebrate success
- Use affirmations
- Exercise!

Notes

Notes

Live Life Now – Rethink 1440

Notes

Live Life Now – Rethink 1440

Notes

GOALS TO DO

#	GOAL	DATE
73	LEARN SITAR	NOW
79	CLIMB 15000' MOUNTAIN	2025
68	QUALIFIED TRAINER	2021
81	TED TALK	2022
93	STAGE TALK 3000PEOPLE	2022
84	SAIL N/S CARIBBEAN	2020
63	LEARN TO KITE SURF	2021
70	SWIM WITH DOLPHINS	2020
51	BEST SELLING 'LIFE' BOOK	2020
56	PARK $10K FOR 1 TALK	2021
72	CATCH A BIG GAME FISH	2021
99	FRANCHISE BUSINESS	2021
106	70 COUNTRIES	2025

Lets Go !

JUNE 2020